Executive Functioning Skills Printables Workbook:
for Students Learning Life Skills

Planning

Name:

Trace the word.

plan

Color in the picture that rhymes with plan.

Color the sentence using rainbow colors.

Sometimes it helps to think out loud when you plan.

Definition:

a method or strategy for achieving a goal

Directions: Circle the correct word that matches the definition.

sidewalk	plan	wait

WRITE IT !!!

plan

Plan...

Mark the picture that shows a plan.

Eat

Work

Play

Name:_____

Trace the word.

waiting

Waiting is when you are inactive or calm in your movements as you expect something to happen.
Remember these words. Read the sentence. Trace the waiting words.

"If I can wait now, I can get that later."

Trace the Waiting Words

soon   later

wait   in the
         future

These are some words to help you wait..

What type of board is this?

 First — work
 Then — play

Directions: Circle the answer that tells the name of this kind of board.

first-then	never	signal

WRITE IT !!!
later
_____
- - - - - - - - - -
_____

What can you do while you wait for something?
Mark 4 things you can do while you wait.

draw or write

play with something

push someone

relax

think about something fun

This page is intentionally blank due to an activity on the next page.

Name:_____

My Schedule

Sometimes planning involves making a schedule. Choose the type of schedule you want. Cut out the template and use the words below to create your own schedule for today or tomorrow.

I will...

My checklist...

Words here

Words here

Words here

Words here

Words here

Reading	Lunch	Recess	Work
Math	Break	Library	Play
Science	Social Skills	Gym	Motor
Social Studies	Cooking	Music	Language Arts
Art	Vocational	Special	Speech

This page is intentionally blank due to an activity on the previous page.

Planning for an Art Project
Sara has 15 minutes in art class to make her art project. She is making a red heart-shaped card. What activities should she do and in what order?

Sara's Art Class Schedule

Place the pictures in the order you want them to go in the schedule.

This page is intentionally blank due to an activity on the previous page.

Organizing

Name:

Trace the word.

organize organize

Mark the word **organize**.

clutter	organize	fill
organ	park	select
sit	orange	run

This girl is trying to organize her locker. Color coding is a good way to organize. She needs help to organize her books by color. Please help her by coloring the books according to the code.

Code:
3 books at the top of the pile = blue
2 books that she is touching = green
2 books on the left of the green books = red
1 book that is remaining = yellow

Name: _____

Fill in the word with rainbow colors.

Draw a line to the same letter in the word organize.

o r g a n i z e

i z e a o r g n

Definition:

To arrange or put things in a structured order.

Directions: Circle the correct word that matches the definition.

| response | city | organize |

In each column, underline the picture of the item that is organized.

   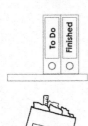  

Organized/Unorganized

Look at the items in front of each student. Mark the picture that shows organized items. Which student is organized?

This page is intentionally blank due to an activity on the next page.

Name: _____

Color in the words.

Organizing My Desk

I can organize my desk and the items in my desk.

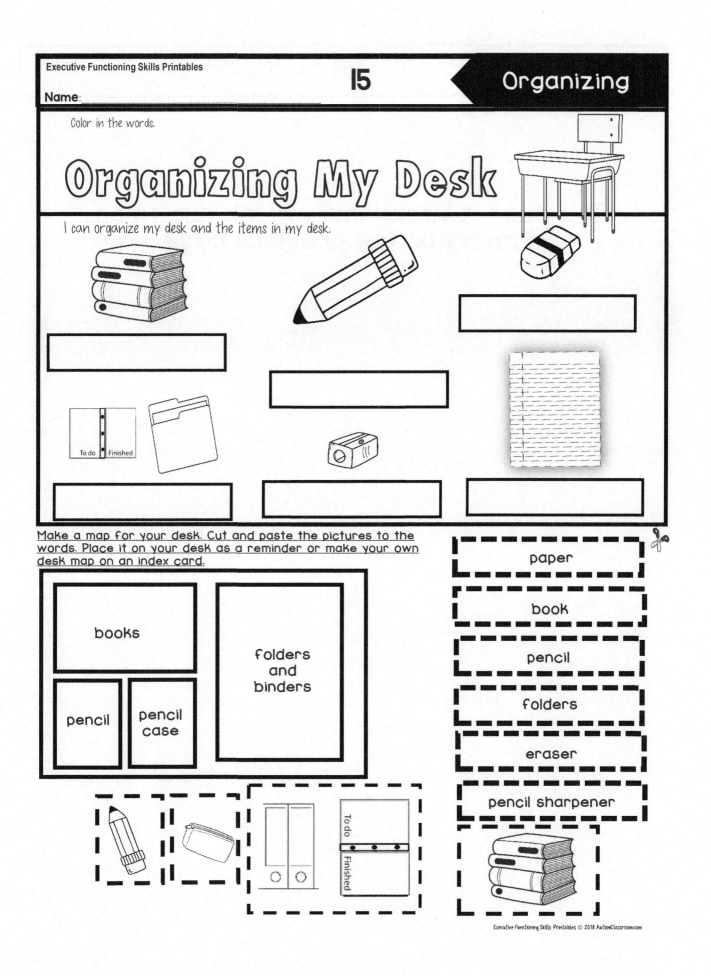

Make a map for your desk. Cut and paste the pictures to the words. Place it on your desk as a reminder or make your own desk map on an index card.

books

folders and binders

pencil

pencil case

paper

book

pencil

folders

eraser

pencil sharpener

To do   Finished

Executive Functioning Skills Printables © 2018 AutismClassroom.com

This page is intentionally blank due to an activity on the previous page.

Name:_____

I Can Organize

Directions: Cut out the cans and organize them on the shelf.

I can organize my groceries!

Groceries

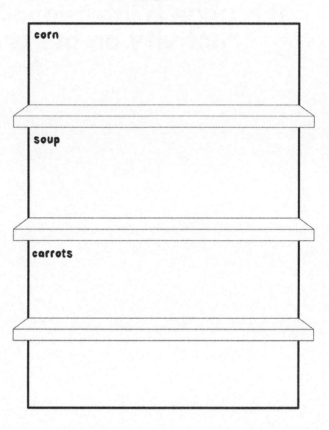

corn

soup

carrots

This page is intentionally blank due to an activity on the previous page.

Time Management

Name: _____

Trace the word.

time

Mark the word **time.**

time	tie	time
rope	want	time
true	time	tap

Is It Time?

John needs to get to gym class at 2:00. Which clock shows when he will be on time?

What Time Does She Do This?

Draw a line to show what time Sally does each activity.

Lunch	Breakfast	Bedtime	Dinner

Name:_____

Timers

Directions: Mark the type of time you like to use.

If I have trouble staying on task, I like to use...

 ☐

  ☐

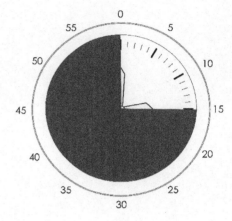

FACT

Timers help us to remember how much time is left or when an activity is over.

  ☐

  ☐

The timer started at 30 minutes. How much time is left on the timer?

30	15	55

This page is intentionally blank due to an activity on the next page.

Name:_____

Smart Watch
A watch can tell the time.
Directions: Cut and paste the correct time to the watch in the square.

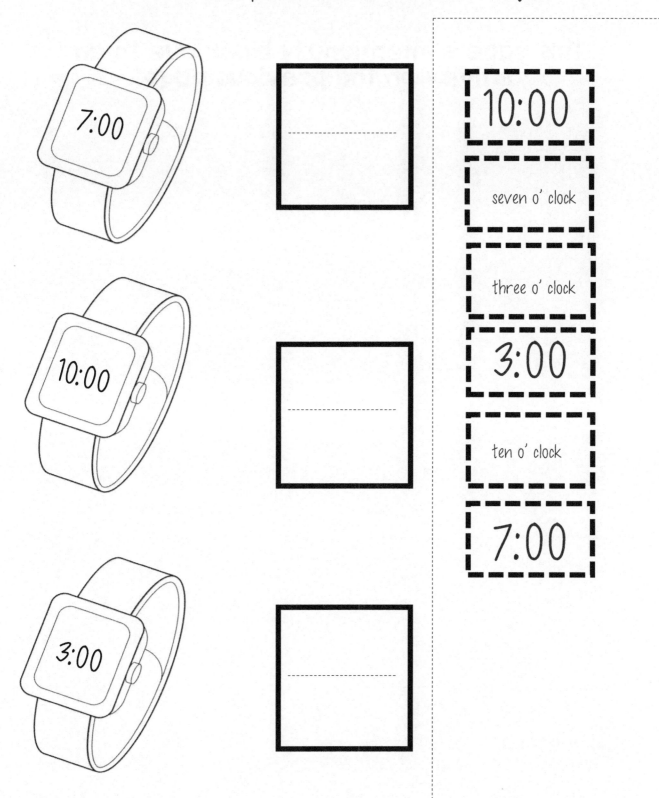

This page is intentionally blank due to an activity on the previous page.

Name:_____

Trace the words.

Task Initiation

Sometimes works tasks are hard and it is difficult to know where to begin. When this occurs think these words to yourself.

This is a difficult task. How can I make this job easier?

  Yes. This will make it easier.

  No. this will not make it easier.

Cut and paste the correct answers above.

Refuse to work.

Make mini goals.

Use a picture schedule.

Get angry.

Share what you want to do by telling another person.

Yell.

Use a timer for each section.

Copy a neighbor.

My checklist...
☑ part 1
☑ part 2
Make a checklist.

Put your head down.

This page is intentionally blank due to an activity on the previous page.

Working Memory

Name:

Repeat After Me

Directions: Repeat the words or tap out the syllables for the word and the phrase. Then, repeat the actions. Color in 'yes' when you are done.

Name: _____

Point to the letters in the word.

remember

FIRST, color these shapes according to the written words inside the shape.

these

NEXT, tap the colors in this order

1. red, yellow, blue
2. green, blue, red
3. red, red, blue
4. blue, yellow, blue

red

green

blue

yellow

LAST, remember which set you tapped correctly. Record a check if you tapped the colors in the correct order.

1	2	3	4

✓ ✓ ✓ ✓

This page is intentionally blank due to an activity on the previous page.

Multi-step Directions

When you have directions that have more than one step, it is helpful to break the task down into smaller pieces. Sometimes you can do one step at a time until the task is finished.

Which way will help you remember large tasks?

Directions: Color in the section or sections that you think will help you with completing a large task.

dogs   both   cats

Graphic Organizer

Page 2:34- 2:36

Write it on the board

First-Then Picture Board

Directions
First, read page 213.
Second, complete the worksheet.
Third, pair up with a peer to answer the questions on page 214.

Sticky Notes

What ways have you tried before?
- ○ Graphic organizer
- ○ Writing the lesson on the board
- ○ Using sticky notes
- ○ Using a first-then board

Letter and Word Search

Circle each letter 'a' you see in the passage.

| | **a** |

I can remember how to do a task by repeating the instructions or repeating the directions. I can also write down what I want to remember on a sticky note.

Mark each time you see 'the' in the passage.

| | **the** |

The next time you need to pay attention, try looking at the person who is talking. You can also listen to what they say and watch the actions of the person. If you want to remember how to do a task, visualize how the task is done before you do the task.

Find the words in the word search.

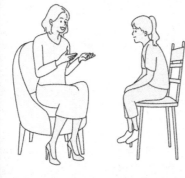

☐ think
☐ pay
☐ attention
☐ listen
☐ look
☐ visualize

```
a  t  t  e  n  t  i  o  n
h  t  p  g  d  f  t  f  n  o
l  l  a  y  c  t  h  t  o  o
v  i  z  u  a  l  i  z  e  l
s  s  e  t  l  s  n  t  l  e
h  t  p  g  d  f  k  t  o  o
o  e  d  a  y  t  q  t  o  k
t  n  y  p  a  y  k  l  k
```

Self-Control

This page is intentionally blank due to an activity on the next page.

Name:_____

Controlling My Actions

People can control their actions. Showing self-control is an important part of growing up. Showing self-control means that you can appropriately manage your emotions, feelings and actions.

Mark the word "control" below.

 captain   cost   too   control   take   shout

Cut and paste the correct answer.

Are these students showing self-control with their actions?

%#*@!

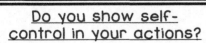

Do you show self-control in your actions?

yes   no
sometimes

| yes | yes | no | no |
| yes | yes | no | no |

This page is intentionally blank due to an activity on the previous page.

Name:_____

Trace the word.

emojis  emojis

nervous

sample	tired	surprised
happy	angry	sad

Cut the emojis and paste them to the corresponding emotion.

This page is intentionally blank due to an activity on the previous page.

Name: _____

Look at each student's face and body language to see how they feel. Match the words at the bottom right of the page to the corresponding words.

sick

hungry

proud

cold

silly

feelings

Read each strategy and color in the box.
I can be in charge of my own emotions.
If I am upset, I can...

☐ Count to five.

☐ Take 3 deep breaths.

☐ Go for a walk.

☐ Think calm thoughts.

☐ Look at pictures of things I like.

True or False?
Even when you feel angry, you can find a calm way to ask for what you want.

I want

☐ true   ☐ false

Cut and paste to the matching word on the left.

sick   hungry   proud

cold   silly

This page is intentionally blank due to an activity on the previous page.

Name:_____

Color in the word.

self-discipline

Self-discipline is the ability to overcome challenges even when temptations are present. Self-discipline helps you to control your impulses to stay focused on what needs to get done to compete tasks. It also helps you to use appropriate skills when working around others. Below are pictures of students. Color in the circle for 'yes' if they are showing self-discipline. Color in 'no' it they are not.

Is this showing self-discipline?

yelling out in class

○ Yes
○ No

Sitting quietly

○ Yes
○ No

○ Yes
○ No

throwing item in the can

getting in someone's face

○ Yes
○ No

What should you do when you are near others?

get too close

keep a safe distance

What are the boys in the picture doing? Mark the correct answer.

○ invading personal space

○ keeping a safe distance

WRITE IT !!!

I can teach myself to

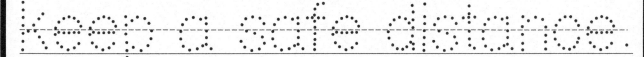

keep a safe distance

This page is intentionally blank.

Impulse Control

Name:

Personal
Bubble

To respect personal space means that you should keep a comfortable distance when you are next to someone or when you are talking to someone. The personal bubble is the space you give when near others. Check the box that goes with the picture.

☐ Yes, this is respecting the personal bubble.
☐ No, this is not respecting the personal bubble.

☐ Yes, this is respecting the personal bubble.
☐ No, this is not respecting the personal bubble.

☐ Yes, this is respecting the personal bubble.
☐ No, this is not respecting the personal bubble.

☐ Yes, this is respecting the personal bubble.
☐ No, this is not respecting the personal bubble.

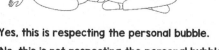
☐ Yes, this is respecting the personal bubble.
☐ No, this is not respecting the personal bubble.

Name:_____

Controlling My Impulses

Cut and paste the pictures to show what you can try when stopping the urge
to say or do something you shouldn't.

These are strategies I can try if I am
thinking of doing something inappropriate.

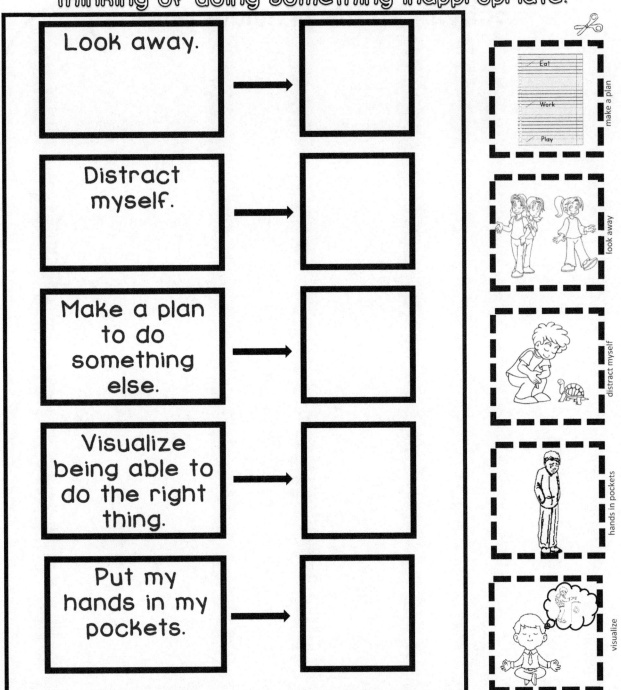

This page is intentionally blank due to an activity on the previous page.

Name:_____

Stop Raging

Directions: Cut on the dashed lines. Put in the
4 other strategies you can do instead of raging.

There are other ways to tell
people your feelings. Some
people use words, sign
language, pictures or a raised
hand to tell their feelings.

Try this.

| use words | push | use a picture | raise hand | yell | sign for help |

This page is intentionally blank due to an activity on the previous page.

Name: _____

Make a Choice

Making good choices is difficult. When you have a hard time with making a choice, try making a choice that is acceptable the adults and to students.

<u>Directions</u>: Make good choices on the choice cards. Mark the good choice.

Choose one.

or

pull your sister's hair   hug your sister

Choose one.

or

get frustrated   ask for help

Choose one.

or

sit in your chair   lean back in your chair

Choose one.

or

leave your seat   stay in your seat

<u>Directions</u>: Trace the letters using rainbow colors.

CALM YOURSELF BY...

1. Sitting upright.

2. Taking a walk.

3. Counting to 10.

Choose
Calm

This page is intentionally blank.

Attention

Name:_____

Trace the word.

Listen

Listen

Mark the words that say **listen.**

attend	listen	respect
child	listen	say
look	reason	listen

Definition:
To hear something with thoughtful attention.

Directions: Circle the correct word.

| look | group | listen |

Directions: Mark what you use to help you listen.

WRITE IT !!!
listen

_____

- - - - - - - - - - - - - -

The word listen <u>begins</u> with which letter?

l   t   y

Name:_____

Visual Schedules

Some people use visual schedules to stay focused on what to do during the school day.
Directions: Place the numbers in order from 1 to 4.

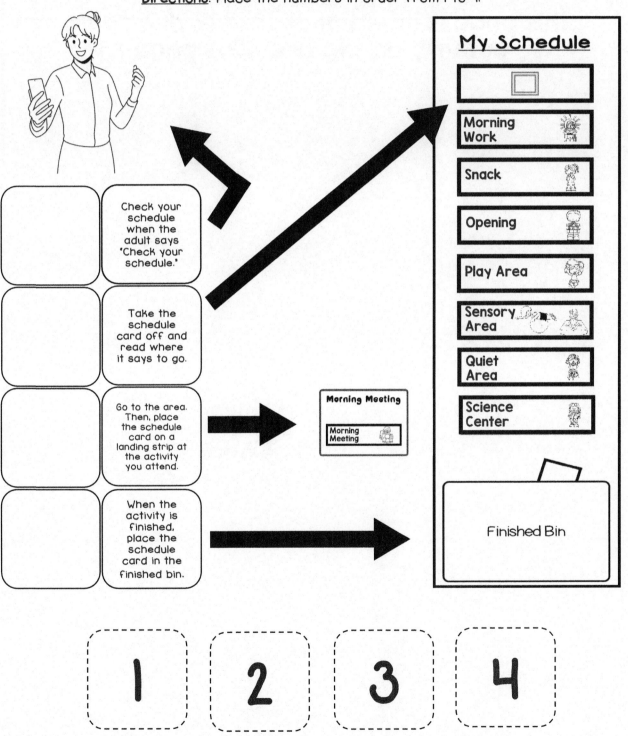

Check your schedule when the adult says "Check your schedule."

Take the schedule card off and read where it says to go.

Go to the area. Then, place the schedule card on a landing strip at the activity you attend.

When the activity is finished, place the schedule card in the finished bin.

Morning Meeting

Morning Meeting

My Schedule

Morning Work

Snack

Opening

Play Area

Sensory Area

Quiet Area

Science Center

Finished Bin

1 2 3 4

This page is intentionally blank due to an activity on the previous page.

Show Listening Skills By Doing These Things

Read each circle. Mark the 3 ways you can show that you are paying attention.

head down

look

listen

raising hand

sticking out tongue

daydreaming

pencil on face

Remember, paying attention means that you are looking and listening.

Staying On Task

Directions: Color 10 of the large circles a light color.
Color 20 of the small circles a dark color.

Mark an X for each circle you color.

light	1 2 3 4 5 6 7 8 9 10

dark	1 2 3 4 5 6 7 8 9 10
	11 12 13 14 15 16 17 18 19 20

   light

o   dark

| All other designs. | your choice

Flexibility

Name:_____

flexibility

Mark the word flexibility

flexibility	county	fair
moon	hair	flexibility
do	flexibility	trunk
flexibility	super	look
sat	flexibility	tune
show	flexibility	feelings

Flexibility Definition

Directions: Mark 3 statements that explain flexibility.

☐ The ability to be easily modified.

☐ Willingness to change or compromise.

☐ Resist working with others.

☐ Showing the quality of being able to change or bend without breaking.

Trace the words that say flexibility.

flexibility

 flexibility   father   family

fleet   flexibility   flexibility

flexibility   fall

Sometimes flexibility is required in the way we respond to others. Empathy can help us respond differently than we have been used to.

You and a classmate are playing a video game together. Your classmate hurts his hand, stops playing and cries. How can you show empathy?

	Yes	No
Say "Are you ok?"	☐	☐
Think about how that would feel if it happened to you.	☐	☐
Keep playing your video game and say nothing.	☐	☐

WRITE IT !!!

empathy

_____
- - - - - - - - - - - - - - -
_____

Name:_____

Trace the words.

Planning a Calendar

Teachers: Add the numbers to the calendar according to this month before making copies.

Make a calendar. Cut the pictures that you need and glue them on the calendar.

Monthly Calendar

Remember that plans can change.

_____
Month

January	February	March	April	May	June
July	August	September	October	November	December

visit grandparent	vacation	no school	weekend	dance	class trip	day trip	babysitter
therapy	birthday	swimming	party	home	visitor	school	½ day

Intentionally Blank (add your pictures here.)

This page is intentionally blank due to an activity on the previous page.

Name:_____

Starting a Non-preferred Activity

Directions: Color the code.

Starting an activity can be difficult. Especially when you do not wat to do the activity. Sometimes our teachers and other adults give us work that we need to do, but do not want to do. Figuring out a way to get motivated will help.

First, I stop what I am doing.

Then, I listen to the directions.

Next, I start the work.

LOOK FOR	DO
A boy who is using his phone.	Color his shoes blue.
A boy listening for his teacher's directions.	Color his shirt orange.
A boy starting his work.	Color his hair brown.

Name:

Trace the letters.

changing plans

Directions: Mark the correct answer.

Sam wants a food item that is no longer available.

What should he do?

Yell or cry.

Choose a different food.

There is a change in the plan.

Tammy is having fun in this activity, then she is asked to leave. *What should she do?*

Stay and not move.

Follow the teacher's directions.

Cathy wanted to use her pen, but his teacher said that only pencils could be used today.

What should she do?

Use a pencil.

Refuse to work.

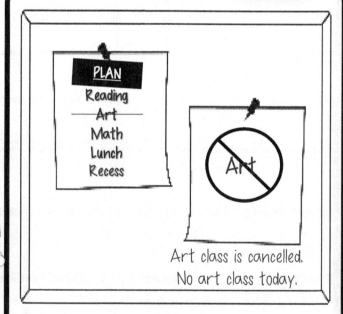

PLAN
Reading
Art
Math
Lunch
Recess

Art class is cancelled. No art class today.

What does this mean?

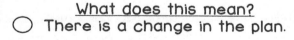

◯ There is a change in the plan.

◯ The plan is the same.

Perseverance

Name:

Trace the word in your favorite colors.

Perseverance

Draw a line to the same letter in the word perseverance.

| p | e | r | s | e | v | e | r | a | n | c | e |

| e | r | p | e | r | a | n | c | e | s | e | v |

Find these words in the word search.

do   not   give   up
   keep   trying

```
d o t e n t i
h t p g n o t
g i v e c t u
k i z u a l p
e k e t l s n
e e p g d f k
p e d a y t q
t r y i n g k
```

Mark 4 ways you can show perseverance.

☐ Give up.

☐ Keep trying.

☐ Try another way.

☐ Ask someone else.

☐ Sit and cry.

A Story About Perseverance

<u>Directions:</u> Cut out the story then place the pages in order from 1 to 6. Staple the booklet together. Read the story.

I Can Work Through My Challenges

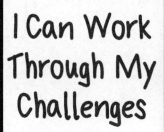

1

Each day I face several challenges.

2

Some challenges are small and some challenges are big. For example, sometimes I can not understand my work assignment. Other times the work seems too hard.

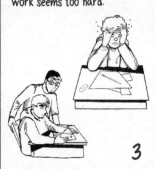

3

Then I remember what my teacher said about working through tough times.

4

My teacher said, "You should keep trying."

5

The next time I face challenges, I will remember to keep trying and not give up.

I WILL TRY.

6

This page is intentionally blank due to an activity on the previous page.

Name: _____

Working to Build Sentences

Directions: Use perseverance to build three unique sentences.

1. _____ .

2. _____ .

3. _____ .

I	blue	store	the
I	red	restaurant	the
I	My	playground	the
We	like	movies	games
our	like to	trampoline	to
my	want	computer	to
in	want to	use	going
out	go	eat	tablet

This page is intentionally blank due to an activity on the previous page.

Name: _____

69

Trace the word.

Work Through It

Sometimes students must work hard through difficult tasks in order to get to something fun.

What items or activities are fun for you?
What are you working to get to do?

I am working
for...

I work for
break

I work for
gum

I work for
phone

I work for
talk time

I work for
computer

I work for
fidget toy

I work for
headphones

I work for
tablet

I work for
special activity

Cut out the letters and paste them in the correct order to spell WORKING.

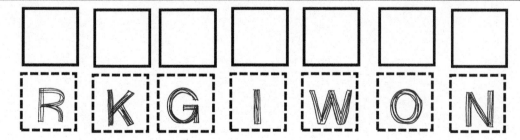

R K G I W O N

This page is intentionally blank due to an activity on the previous page.

Transitioning

This page is intentionally blank due to an activity on the next page.

Name:_____

Trace the word.

change

change

What is the definition of change?

☐ To make different or to become different.

☐ To stay the same.

What things can change?

Directions: Paste in the correct word to go with the picture.

time → ☐

activities → ☐

answers → ☐

schedule → ☐

groups → ☐

time | activities | answers | schedule | groups

This page is intentionally blank due to an activity on the previous page.

Name:_____

Starting a New Assignment

Let's Go!

What Can I Do?

Stop what I am doing.
Put away what I am doing.
Start new assignment.
Re-read the instructions.
State instructions in my own words.
Ask for help if I need it.

<u>Directions</u>: Cut out each phrase and match it to the same phrase above.

Stop what I am doing.
Put away what I am doing.
Start new assignment.
Re-read the instructions.
State instructions in my own words.
Ask for help if I need it.

This page is intentionally blank due to an activity on the previous page.

Working Until My Scheduled Break

Cut out the picture and match the picture to the card.

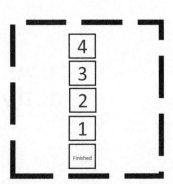

Doing My Work

I like to play with my tablet but I have to wait until my work is done. On my break, I can play with my tablet. Once I do my work, I can use the tablet.

A Count Down Board

I am allowed to listen to my music on my headphones after my work is complete. My teacher uses a count down board to show me when the headphones are finished. The numbers come off of the board 4,3,2,1, and then the headphones are finished. Sometimes I still want to use them, but I know it is time to take them off.

Asking For a Break

Things are better when I remember the appropriate way to ask for a break. When I am working, I do my best. I stay seated for a sit down task and I stand up for a standing task. I keep a quiet voice and I ask for a break by raising my hand or I wait my schedule says it is break time.

This page is intentionally blank due to an activity on the previous page.

Name:_____

Transition Cues

It is good to know the words and phrases that can let you know when it is time to end one activity and begin another activity. Ending one activity and beginning another activity is called making a transition. See the pictures below to find out the different ways that you can know when a change in the activity (transition) is going to happen.

What can signal that it is time for a transition?

environmental cues (everyone else is lining up)

the daily schedule

my personal schedule

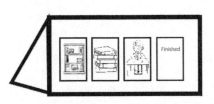

an activity schedule

the teacher's words

Match under the correct picture. (Match to the same words.)

| the daily schedule | my personal schedule | the teacher's words |

| environmental cues (everyone else is lining up) | an activity schedule |

This page is intentionally blank due to an activity on the previous page.

Problem Solving

Name:_____

Trace the word.

Problem Solving

Steps To Solving Problems

1 State the Problem

2 List Possible Solutions

3 Write the Impact of Those Solutions

I keep losing my pencil.

-look for it
-borrow a pencil
-get a pencil case
-keep a spare pencil

1. I can finish my work on time.

2. I will be prepared.

3. I will be more responsible.

Directions: Draw a line from number 1 to step 1, from number 2 to step 2, from number 3 to step 3.

| 3 | 1 | 2 |

One Way to Solve the Problem of Unorganized Papers

A folder system can help organize papers.

To do   Finished

How can a student solve the problem of a messy folder? (Circle the correct answer.)

a. Put the work to be done on the left side and put the finished work on the right side.

b. Put all of the papers in random order.

Name:

Is this a Good Strategy?

John has a problem controlling his impulses. What should he do?

Make a social story to remind about controlling impulses.	
Use role play to act out situations beforehand. 	
Cry and drop things on the floor. 	
Carry a goal list and check the list before doing anything impulsive.	
Use self-talk to remind yourself of what you are supposed to do.	

Directions: Cut out the answers to tell if it is a good strategy or if it is not a good strategy.

No, not a good strategy.	Yes, a good strategy.
No, not a good strategy.	Yes, a good strategy.
No, not a good strategy.	Yes, a good strategy.
No, not a good strategy.	Yes, a good strategy.
No, not a good strategy.	Yes, a good strategy.

This page is intentionally blank due to an activity on the previous page.

Name:

Trace the word.

Visualize It

I can see it.

Did you know that you can try to solve a problem by visualizing the solution. Make a mental picture in your head of how it should be. Think through the solution in your mind before attempting to solve the problem.

How can you problem solve?
Choose 3 answers.

Picture the solution in your head.

Think of a solution and try to see how it might work out.

Give up.

Visualize a solution.

Word Search

First, visualize how to solve this problem. Then, solve this problem.

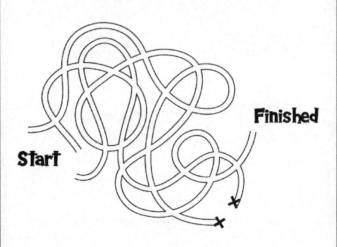

Start

Finished

Name:

Thinking of Strategies When Feeling Anxious

Anxiety is the feeling of being worried, nervous or uneasy about an event or about something with an uncertain outcome. One way to ease anxiety is to develop a script or plan to deal with the event. Students can create these plans with an adult at home or at school.

This would help me...

In the <u>hallway</u> I can...

Go out in the hallway before the bell rings to avoid the crowd. ☐

Go out in the hallway after the crowd. ☐

Travel with a peer that I know. ☐

Wear earphones in the hallway. ☐

At an <u>assembly</u> I can...

Sit in the back of the room. ☐

Sit by the door. ☐

Wear earphones. ☐

Carry a fidget. ☐

In the <u>cafeteria</u> I can...

Be the first in line to go through the lunch line. ☐

Sit near the door. ☐

Sit with a set group of people. ☐

See the menu choices ahead of time. ☐

Directions: Mark which 2 activities calm you the best when you are feeling anxious?

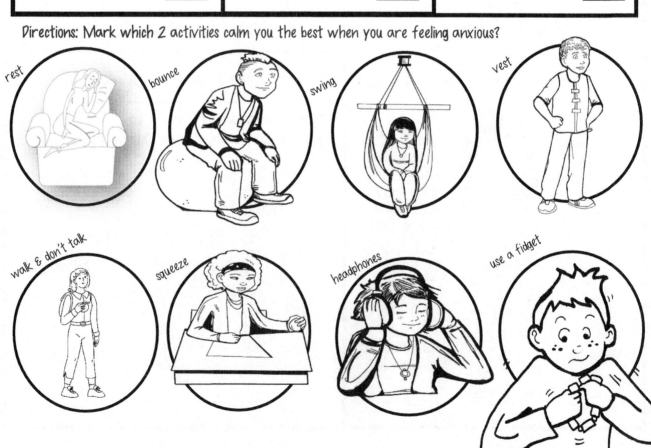

rest   bounce   swing   vest

walk & don't talk   squeeze   headphones   use a fidget

This page is intentionally blank.

THANK YOU FOR YOUR PURCHASE.

AutismClassroom.com offers tips, books and resources for Special Education and General Education. We make materials to bring out the best in your students.

  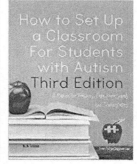 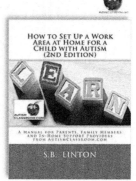

Looking for workbooks to encourage and build skills?

Try our workbook series!

Workbooks for:
- Language Skills
- Toilet Training Skills
- Imitation Skills
- Play Skills
- Behavior Skills
- Social Skills

- Numbers
- ABC's
- Shapes

Click Here

Website: www.autismclassroom.com
Instagram: www.Instagram.com/autismclassroom

Some of the clip art and fonts were created by the following artists.

Illumismart
Educlips
Rossey's Jungle

Printed in Great Britain
by Amazon

41240554R00051